TO

_____

FROM

Chuck Greenwood

Henny Penny

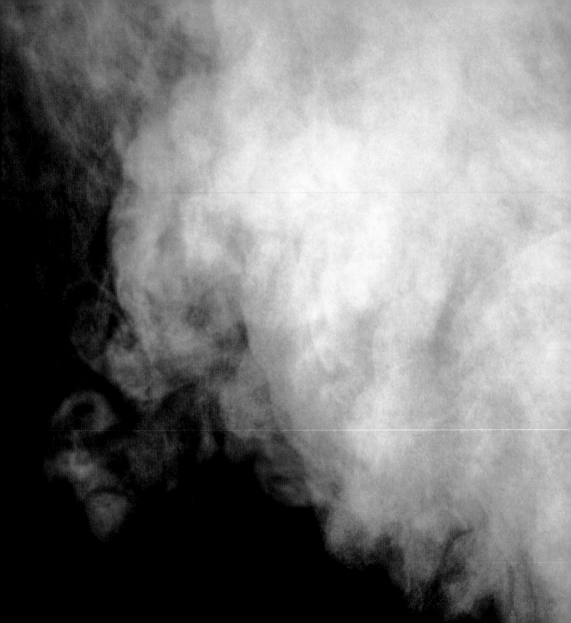

212°

the extra degree

Sam Parker & Mac Anderson

PHOTO CREDITS:

Dick Durrance II *(www.drinkerdurrance.com)* page 26

Bruce Heinemann *(www.theartofnature.com)* pages 30, 42, 48

Ken Jenkins *(www.kenjenkins.com)* page 92

Rich Nickel *(www.richnickeldesign.com)* pages 32, 64, 96, 98

Todd Reed *(www.toddreedphoto.com)* page 74

Steve Terrill *(www.terrillphoto.com)* pages 36, 56, 68, 100

Design: Rich Nickel
Editor: Michelle Sedas

Printed and bound in the United States of America

www.simpletruths.com

212°
the extra degree

contents

8 .... Introduction

24 .... 212° Thoughts & Facts

46 .... 212° Stories

84 .... 212° Actions

92 .... 212° Reflections

At 2 1 1 degrees, water is hot.

At 2 1 2 degrees, it boils.

And with boiling water,
comes steam.

And steam can power
a locomotive.

ONE
DEGREE

Raising the temperature of water by one extra degree means the difference between something that is simply very hot and something that generates enough force to power a machine — a beautiful, uncomplicated metaphor that ideally should feed our every endeavor — consistently pushing us to make the extra effort in every task we undertake. 212° serves as a forceful drill sergeant with its motivating and focused message while adhering to a scientific law — a natural law. It reminds us that seemingly small things can make tremendous differences. So simple is the analogy that you can stop reading right now, walk away with the opening thought firmly planted in your mind, and benefit from it for the rest of your life.

That's the purpose of this book — to help you internally define and take ownership of the most fundamental principle behind achieving life results beyond your expectations — a simple idea with a singular focus — an actionable focus.

212°

It's this dramatic — three numbers joined together to form one, crystallizing a message that absolutely assures life -altering, positive results for those who choose to apply it.

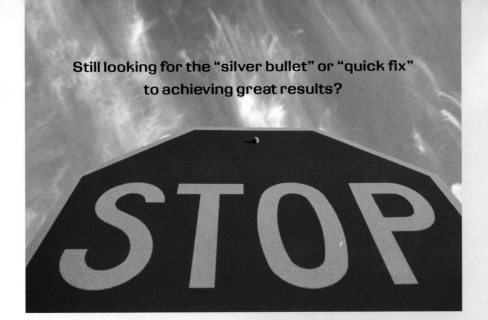

Still looking for the "silver bullet" or "quick fix"
to achieving great results?

Reams of material are written and taught with an approach to reaching an end by close to effortless means — and more will be written. Advertising messages continually promote methods of achieving end results with little or no effort. And this material and these messages are so effective that in many cases people will work harder to avoid the extra effort than to actually apply the effort that will produce the originally desired outcome.

Great materials with solid approaches to results have also been created and taught. Unfortunately, action on the part of the reader/student in so many cases is the missing ingredient. And for those individuals who do take action, there are even a smaller number who make the extra effort necessary to reach the desired results that were originally set to be achieved. Books are purchased, programs are attended, and clubs are joined with wonderful intentions of putting forth the effort to achieve — only to end in another block of time invested half-heartedly with appropriately corresponding results.

why?

Why do you enter into any activity with anything but a

commitment

to achieve your objective of that activity — not a desire to

achieve your objective, but a commitment?

212° is not only a message of action — it's a message of **persistent and additional action** — the continual application of heat (effort) to whatever task or activity you undertake in order to achieve not only the primary objective you seek, but to reap the **exponential rewards** that are possible by applying one extra degree of effort.

How many opportunities have you missed because you were not aware of the possibilities that would occur if you applied a small amount of effort beyond what you normally do?

People develop personal habits toward action and rarely attempt to develop them further and continually. Unless someone engages in frequent self-review or an external source (a friend, a book, a manager, a spouse, a parent, an article, etc.) brings something to one's attention, a person will continue throughout life making very small improvements if any at all.

Now you're aware of "212° — the extra degree." No longer will you be able to do only what is required of you and only what is expected of you. Because with this awareness comes responsibility — to yourself and to others. And, again...

You are now
aware.

You now have a target for everything you do...

212°

You may not always be able to turn up the heat and hit the boiling point, but that doesn't mean you shouldn't make the attempt. It's what you'd advise others to do and it's what we should teach our children.

211° can serve a purpose but 212° is the extra degree — the extra degree that will bring exponential results — exponential results to you and those you touch throughout your days.

There are no real secrets to success. Success in anything has one fundamental aspect — effort. To achieve exponential results requires additional effort. Take your courses. Read your books. Listen to your tapes. But take action. **Take action with commitment.** Then, when you're ready for exponential results, apply the extra effort. Sometimes you'll have immediate exponential results and sometimes you'll realize the benefits of your extra effort much farther down the road. Regardless, in many cases, it may only be that one extra push that gets you ten times the results you were attempting to originally obtain.

Pace your expectations and operate at your new target.

At 211 degrees, water is hot.

At 212 degrees, it boils.

And with boiling water,
comes steam.

And steam can power
a locomotive.

It's your life.

You

are responsible for your results.

It's time to turn up the heat.

From this day forward, commit to operating at 212° in everything you do. Etch it into your thinking — into your being. Apply it to your actions. It guarantees to increase your results positively and, in so many cases, increase your results exponentially.

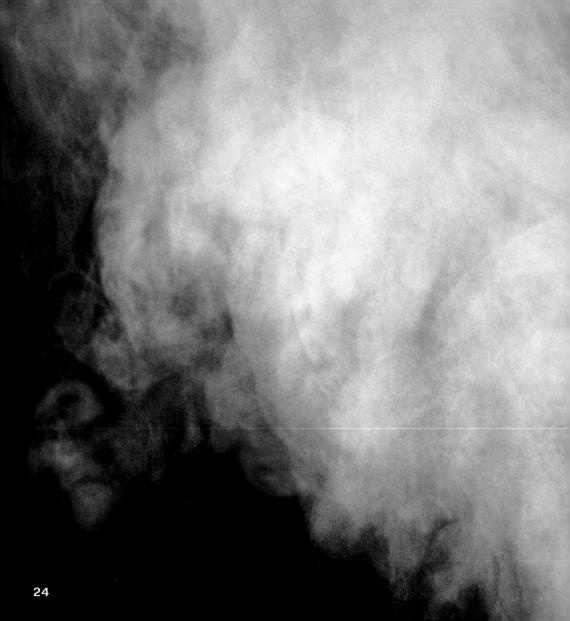

212°
thoughts
& facts

Professional golf tournaments are comprised of four rounds of 18 holes played over a four-day period (72 holes total). There are four major tournaments each year — The U.S. Open, The British Open, The PGA Championship, and The Masters. The average margin of victory between 1980 and 2004 (25 years) in ALL tournaments combined was less than three strokes — less than a one-stroke difference per day. From 2000 through 2004 (five years), the winner across all tournaments took home an average of 76% more in prize dollars than the second place finisher.

The average
margin of victory
for the last 25 years
in all major tournaments
combined was
less than
three strokes.

Courage is fear holding

n a minute longer.

GEORGE S. PATTON
AMERICAN SOLDIER & GENERAL
1885 - 1945

Many of life's failures
are men who did not realize
how close they were to
success when they
gave up.

THOMAS EDISON
AMERICAN INVENTOR
1847 - 1931

Inches make a champion.

VINCE LOMBARDI
HALL OF FAME FOOTBALL COACH
1913 - 1970

To get what we've never had, we must do what we've never done.

ANONYMOUS

The margin for victory between an Olympic Gold Medal and no medal at all is extremely small.

During the 2004 Summer Olympic Games, the margin of victory was:

Men's 200 meter Freestyle (swimming)	1.42	seconds
Women's 200 meter Freestyle	0.59	seconds
Men's 800 meter (running)	0.71	seconds
Women's 800 meter	0.13	seconds
Men's Long Jump	28	centimeters
Women's Long Jump	11	centimeters

The drops of rain
make a hole in the stone
not by violence,
but by oft falling.

LUCRETIUS
ROMAN PHILOSOPHER
c. 50 B.C.

Triumph often is nearest when defeat seems inescapable.

B. C. FORBES
FOUNDER & PUBLISHER
FORBES MAGAZINE
1880 - 1954

Horse racing's classic races include the Kentucky Derby, the Preakness, and the Belmont Stakes. A horse that wins each of these races in a single year is considered a Triple Crown winner — an unofficial title held by only 11 horses in the history of the sport. The Kentucky Derby and the Preakness last approximately two minutes with the Belmont finishing at just over two and a half minutes. The average margin of victory between 1998 and 2002 over each of the Triple Crown races combined (15 races in all) was less than 2.5 lengths. Six races were won by less than a length (40%).

The average payout to the winner in these races was nearly **400% more** than the horse that placed second.

The line between failure
and success is so fine that we...
are often on the line and
do not know it.

How many a man has
thrown up his hands at a time
when a little more effort,
a little more patience,
would have achieved success.

A little more effort,
and what seemed hopeless
failure may turn
to glorious success.

ELBERT HUBBARD
AMERICAN WRITER & BUSINESS PERSON
1856 - 1915

In the
confrontation
between the
stream and
the rock,
the stream
always wins...
not through
strength
but by
perseverance.

H. JACKSON BROWN

The average margin for victory for the past 10 years has been 1.54 seconds.

The prize money for second place was less than half the winner's.

Two of auto racing's premier events are the Daytona 500 and the Indianapolis 500. Each takes roughly three to three and a half hours to complete. In the last ten years of each race combined, the winner took the checkered flag by an average margin of 1.54 seconds and took home $1,278,813 in first prize money. **The average prize for second place was $621,321 — a difference of $657,492.**

212°
stories

212°
service

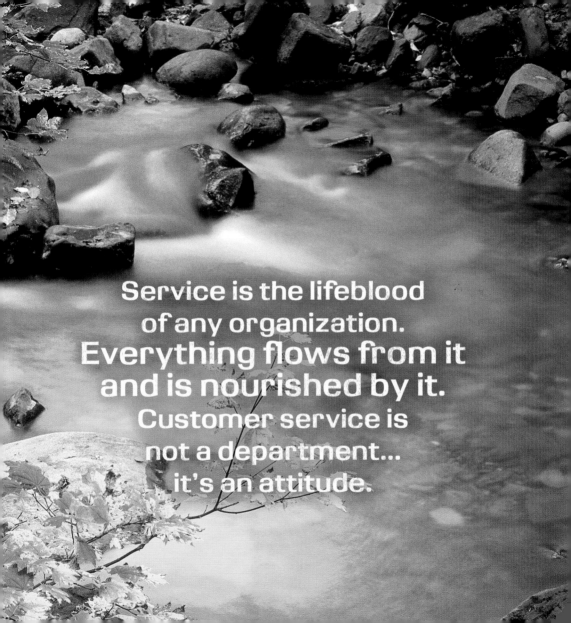

Service is the lifeblood
of any organization.
Everything flows from it
and is nourished by it.
Customer service is
not a department...
it's an attitude.

212°service

Many companies talk the talk when it comes to customer service, but most fall short when it comes to delivering it on a consistent basis. One company that truly understands what 212° service is all about is The Ritz-Carlton Hotel Company. It's the only service company to twice capture the prestigious Malcolm Baldridge National Quality Award. Whenever possible, employees greet guests by name, they record details about guest preferences — from favorite drinks to entertainment — and use the information to custom-tailor future stays. They also attempt to solve every problem they encounter, and any Ritz-Carlton employee can spend up to $2,000 to resolve a problem on the spot.

For the 59-hotel luxury chain, it starts with hiring positive, empathetic workers who are eager to please. Next comes 20 days of training before they even set foot in the hotel.

Once they start, however, every employee carries a small card with the company's 20 core values. What happens next separates Ritz-Carlton from the "Ritz-Carlton wannabes." Every day, all of the company's 25,000 employees partake in a 15-minute session to discuss (and reinforce) one of those core values. What Ritz-Carlton has learned is that service doesn't just happen because of a prestigious name, but is delivered by reinforcing values and attitudes — on a daily basis! This, in their opinion, is the only way to ensure that values are transferred into actions and behaviors throughout the organization.

212°
attitude

The only thing that stands
between a person and what they
want in life is
the will to try it
and the faith to believe
it possible.

I've been an entrepreneur for over 30 years, and I've come to realize that the difference in success or failure is not how you look, how you dress, or how you're educated. It's how you think!

212°
attitude

Early in my career, I was the vice president of sales for a food company. One time I was in Detroit hiring a sales person for the market. We had lined up eight appointments for the day, and the morning had been a bust.

I looked up and my 1 o'clock appointment was standing at the door. He was a tall, good-looking guy, and I remember thinking, "This could be the one." We talked for about 15 minutes, and I asked a question I always ask, "What will you be doing five years from now?" I'll never forget his answer. He said, "Mr. Anderson, the way these appointments have been going, I might still be interviewing!" Well, that wasn't exactly what I wanted to hear. We talked for a few more minutes and I excused him.

Then I looked up and my 2 o'clock was there ... a short guy with a wrinkled sport coat. He walked over and gave me a confident handshake, and a few minutes later I asked the same question, "What are you going to be doing five years from now?" He looked me right in the eye and said, "Mr. Anderson, I'm going to be working for you. This job fits my skills and my needs to a tee. I don't just think, I know I can sell your product in this market. And furthermore, if you don't like my performance after thirty days, you don't owe me a cent."

Well, you could have knocked me over with a feather! He had just made me an offer I couldn't refuse. But the offer had nothing to do with the money I might save; it had everything to do with his unwavering passion and belief he could do it. Within a year, Bob was the number one sales person in the company.

The power of a 212° attitude can be unstoppable.

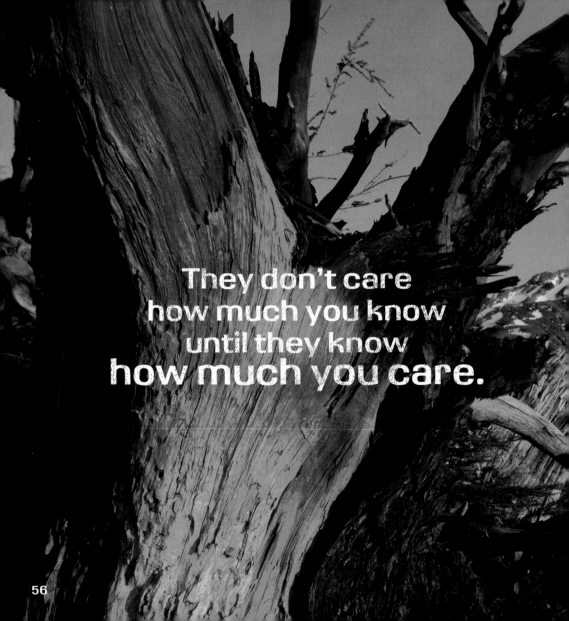

212°
leadership

212° leadership

O N MARCH 18, 2003, I turned on *Good Morning America* while eating breakfast. Charles Gibson was interviewing General Earl Hailston, the commanding general of Marine Forces Central Command. The general was waiting with his troops just a few miles off the border of Iraq ... waiting to go to war. General Hailston is the only general in the armed forces who had enlisted and came up through the ranks, and as he spoke, I was impressed by his humble and caring attitude.

Toward the end of the interview, his answer to a question touched me deeply. When Charles asked him if he had any hobbies outside his work, the general said, "Yes, I love photography, especially taking photos of my men." He shared that while he had been waiting for the past few days he would take photos of his men, and at night he would e-mail the photos with a brief note to their mothers back in the USA. Charles asked if he could see a sample of a letter, and the general walked into his tent, turned on his computer:

> Dear Mrs. Johnson,
>
> I thought you might enjoy seeing this picture of your son. He is doing great. I also wanted you to know that you did a wonderful job of raising him. You must be very proud. I can certainly tell you that I'm honored to serve with him in the U.S. Marines.
>
> General Earl Hailston

Wow! I had goose bumps as I watched. I then watched Charles randomly interview a few of General Hailston's men. You could feel the genuine love and respect that they all had for their leader. You may have heard the quote ... "They don't care how much you know until they know how much you care." Well, here's a man who truly understood what 212° leadership is all about.

212° kindness

It is one of the most beautiful
compensations in life...
we can never help another
**without helping
ourselves.**

RALPH WALDO EMERSON

ONE OF MY FAVORITE THINGS to do is waking up early on Sunday morning, getting the Sunday paper, making a hot cup of coffee, and kicking back to read about what's going on in the world. It's my quiet time ... my time alone to reflect and relax.

212° kindness

One Sunday morning about halfway through my little ritual, I spotted a headline that read "Graduating Student Credits His 'Angel'" ... and I began to read. A young man who was graduating from college told the story about how Oral Lee Brown was his "Real Life Angel." In 1987 Brown, a real estate agent in Northern California, saw a young girl in her neighborhood begging for money. When she went to the school the girl had claimed to attend, Brown couldn't find her, but that day she made a decision that would change the lives of many other children forever. She adopted an entire first-grade class in one of Oakland's lowest-performing schools, and she pledged that she personally would pay for anyone who wanted to attend college.

This would be a great story even if Oral Lee Brown were independently wealthy; however, it is a much greater story considering she was a former cotton picker from Mississippi, making $45,000 a year and raising two children of her own.

Brown lived up to her pledge. Since 1987, she's personally saved $10,000 a year while also raising donations for her "adopted first-grade kids." And because of her tremendous act of unselfish love, children who could have been "swallowed by the streets" are now graduating from college to pursue their dreams.

We all seek our purpose in life. Most of us wonder how we can make a positive difference during our brief time on this earth. But asking and doing are different things. Oral Lee Brown embodies what 212° kindness is all about.

212°

commitment

If you will spend
an extra hour each day
of study in your chosen field,
you will be a national expert
in that field in five years
or less.

EARL NIGHTINGALE

NOT TOO LONG AGO, I had the opportunity to hear Jim Cathcart speak to a corporate audience. Jim is a good friend, and a great speaker. He told the story of how listening to a radio program over 25 years ago changed his life forever, and with his permission I'd like to share it with you.

212°
commitment

In 1972, Jim was working at the Little Rock, Arkansas, Housing Authority making $525 a month, with a new wife and baby at home, no college degree, no past successes, and not much hope for the foreseeable future.

One morning, he was sitting in his office listening to the radio, to a program called "Our Changing World" by Earl Nightingale, who was known as "the Dean of Personal Development." That day, Nightingale, in his booming voice, said something that would change Jim's life forever: "If you will spend an extra hour each day of study in your chosen field, you will be a national expert in that field in five years or less."

Jim was stunned, but the more he thought about it the more it made sense. Although he had never given a speech, he had always wanted to help people grow in areas of personal development motivation. He began his quest to put Nightingale's theory to the test by reading books and listening to tapes whenever he could. He also started exercising and joined a self-improvement study group. He persisted through weeks of temptations to quit, just by doing a little more each day to further his goal. Within six months he had learned more than he had in his few years of college, and he began to believe he could turn his goal of becoming a motivational speaker into reality. All the hard work, the discipline, and study paid off. Jim now has delivered more than 2,500 speeches worldwide and has won every major award in the speaking industry.

Just like companies have market value, so do people. In the simplest terms, your market value increases by knowing and doing more. You see, Jim really understood one of my favorite laws in life ... you cannot get what you've never had unless you're willing to do what you've never done.

He understood the power of 212° commitment.

212°
belief

Belief fuels
enthusiasm, and
**enthusiasm explodes
into passion.**
It fires our souls and
lifts our spirits.

WHAT HAPPENS WHEN you believe something with all your heart? Belief fuels enthusiasm, and enthusiasm explodes into passion. It fires our souls and lifts our spirits.

212°belief

In 1991, when Successories hired Tim Dumler as a corporate account manager, he shared his goal of becoming number one in the company with his manager, Neil Sexton. But Neil, quite frankly, had serious doubts that Tim could make it through the first month, much less be number one.

Neil's first two interviews with Tim were conducted over the phone, and he passed those with flying colors. But when Neil met Tim for the first time, he was shocked when Tim told him he was legally blind. He began to lose his sight when he was in the third grade from a rare disease called macular degeneration. Tim acknowledged he would have problems entering orders into the computers, but he had a possible solution. He told Neil about a machine that he could hook up to magnify the letters on the screen to two inches high. Tim was willing to buy it if he could have the job.

After the conversation, Neil came to my office and explained the situation. I said, "Neil, let's give him a chance," but I must admit, I had serious doubts that Tim could do it.

Well, we were dead wrong. We grossly underestimated Tim's passion and his determination to succeed. Even though it took him much longer to enter the orders, Tim made it work. He came in early. He worked late. Whatever it took, he did it.

In 1991, Tim's first year, he was number one out of ten experienced corporate sales reps, with over $500,000 in sales. In 1994 he was number one again with $700,000, and again in 1997 with $950,000. His customers loved him because when you can't see, you become a great listener. His peers loved him because of his caring, positive attitude.

He was certainly an inspiration to me, too. I asked him one time, "Tim, how do you stay so positive?" He said, "Mac, it's unfortunate that I'm visually impaired, but I have to tell you that fighting through the adversity has made me a better person. I have come to realize that I have a lot more than I don't have. I love my family, my work, and the people I work with. I've been blessed in many ways."

Tim's 212° belief enabled him to overcome many obstacles, and propelled him to success.

"Whether you think
you can, or think
you can't...
you're right."

HENRY FORD

212°

focus

Having a simple, clearly defined goal can capture the imagination and inspire passion. It can **cut through the fog** like a beacon in the night.

212° focus is critical to your success in business ... and also in life. I must admit, however, that this is something that took me a while to learn. "More is better" sounds reasonable, but I've learned the opposite is usually true. Less, I've discovered, is usually more. (This book is a good example.)

212°focus

The reason, of course, is that there is something powerful about laser-like focus. **Having simple, clearly defined goals** can cut through the fog like a beacon in the night.

In 1981, Jan Carlzon had just been named the CEO of Scandinavian Airlines. His company was in trouble. They had just been ranked by a consumer poll as the worst airline in the world. Last in service, last in dependability, and last in profits as a percentage of sales. Yet one year later, in the same poll, they were ranked number one in all three categories. What happened?

Carlzon had decided to focus on what he thought was the most critical issue ... serving the customer. He wanted to keep it simple: identify every contact between the customer and the employee and treat that contact as "a moment of truth." He set out to let his people know the importance of that moment ... the captain, the ticket agent, the baggage handler, the flight attendant. "Every moment, every contact," he said, "must be as pleasant and as memorable as possible." He determined that he had approximately ten million customers each year, and on average each customer made contact with five of his people for approximately 15 seconds at a time. Carlzon felt that what happened in these 50 million contacts would determine the fate of his company.

He set out to share his vision with his 20 thousand employees. He knew the key was to empower the front line. Let them make the decisions and take action, because they were Scandinavian Airlines during those 15 seconds. He now had 20 thousand people who were energized and ready to go because they focused on one very important thing ... making every moment count. Carlzon made it happen with 212° focus; and you can too.

212°
perseverance

Perseverance
is not a long race:
It is many short races,
one after another.

WALTER ELLIOT

Carl Mays, a speaker and author, recently shared an amazing story that I think captures the essence of 212° perseverance. I want to share it with you.

212°
perseverance

In December 1914, departing from South Georgia, an island in the Atlantic Ocean, Ernest Shackleton led a crew of 27 men in a quest to cross Antarctica on foot, the last-known unclaimed prize in exploration annals. As they drew within 85 miles of the continent, their ship was trapped by unusually thick ice. Originally called *Polaris*, the ship had been renamed *Endurance* by Shackleton, a term derived from his family motto, *Fortitudine Vincimus*, which means "by endurance we conquer." This name proved to be prophetic.

Frozen fast for ten months, the trapped ship was eventually crushed and destroyed by the increasing pressure. Forced to abandon the ship, the men salvaged their lifeboats, camped on the ice for five months, and hiked to navigable waters. Amazingly, Shackleton and every crew member survived for 20 months in one of the most vicious regions of the world. They overcame extreme cold, breaking ice floes, leopard seal attacks, a shortage of food and drinking water, and finally two open boat trips.

The most remarkable of the small boat trips was a treacherous 800-mile ocean crossing back to South Georgia by Shackleton and a few of the men. Today, that achievement is considered one of the greatest accomplishments in nautical history. After arriving at South Georgia, Shackleton led his team across the rugged, icy mountains, reached the island's remote whaling station, organized a rescue team, and went back for the others.

The miraculous outcome against horrendous odds was attributed to Shackleton's leadership. When interviewed later, every member of the crew said he highly respected and admired

212°
perseverance

Shackleton throughout the entire two-year ordeal. Shackleton never doubted they would survive and he communicated this confidence to the others. But his optimism was mixed with realism. When it became clear the *Endurance* could not withstand the pressure of the ice, he made plans to abandon ship, set up camp, and search for additional possibilities. When they journeyed across the ice and Shackleton realized the need to discard weight, one of the first things to go was his valuable heirloom gold watch, which the men knew he greatly treasured. In the lifeboat journey through the frigid stormy sea, he daringly stood in the stern of the small craft and meticulously guided its course.

Shackleton maintained cohesion and cooperation among the men. He constantly emphasized, "We are one — we live or die together." He made it clear that he was in command, but he was always open to others' opinions and asked for input and suggestions. He led open discussions each evening and helped build social bonds among the men. He stressed courtesy and mutual respect. Everyone, including Shackleton, worked side by side and performed chores.

Shackleton defused anger. He wisely handled power struggles and dissidents before they could take hold, even sharing his tent with the potentially biggest dissenter. He had to alter short-term objectives and keep the men's energy on these objectives while never losing focus of the long-term goals. He found ways to lighten things up with humor and made sure there were always little successes to celebrate. His methods and actions eliminated what could have been devastating anxiety and despair among the men.

In the end, he knew that survival depended on a bold act, literally a do-or-die act, which was the attempt to reach an outpost by crossing 800 miles of tempestuous seas in an open boat. He took the chance. As a result, all 28 men not only survived, but also became the epitome of the rewards that can come from belief, creativity, and 212° perseverance.

212°
actions

Ideas for implementing the 212° mindset in your life are suggested in the following pages. These are specific ways for you to begin taking 212° action right now — this week.

They're just the beginning for you. Grab hold of one or two and begin (or start with your own). Once you start, it'll be difficult for you to act in any other way. 212° will become a wonderful new habit in your world — a backdrop to all that you do — a habit that will create fantastic life results for you and help you serve as an influence to all those people around you.

Remember...

With awareness comes responsibility...

responsibility to act.

As a
friend

Choose to visit or talk with one extra friend **each week** and create 52 additional discussions among friends for the year.

Do something helpful and unexpected for one friend each week of the year and plant more than 50 additional possibilities of influence.

As a
parent

Wake and act **each day** with the understanding that your actions will be absorbed by your children ... and your children will grow to be contributing adults to the level of your influence.

Add an extra 15 minutes each day to the time you invest with your children — an equivalent of more than two weeks each year at work. Imagine the exponentially positive effect of investing two extra weeks each year exclusively in the development of your children.

At
work

Make the extra contact each day ...

a sales call ... a customer ...

a brief discussion with a colleague ...

an encouraging talk with a member of your team.

With contact comes opportunity.

At the end of a year, you'll have opened more than

200 additional doors of possibility.

And then
some...

The secret to anyone's success is what I call "And-then-some syndrome." The power of these words is captured in a short essay written by Carl Holmes.

And then some... these three little words are the secret to success. They are the difference between average people and top people in most companies. The top people always do what is expected ... and then some. They are thoughtful of others; they are considerate and kind ... and then some. They meet their responsibilities fairly and squarely ... and then some. They are good friends and helpful neighbors ... and then some. They can be counted on in an emergency ... and then some. I am thankful for people like this, for they make the world a better place. Their spirit of service is summed up in these three little words ... and then some.

212°
reflections

Practice
kindness

You see the opportunity. You are aware.

But you're busy.

"I need to be somewhere, doing something,

otherwise I'd help."

"Someone else will do it."

"Someone else will pick it up."

"Someone else can handle it."

"It's not my responsibility."

212° thought

A person struggles. You help. A door needs to be opened. You open it. A piece of trash is in your path. You pick it up and throw it away. A child needs some extra attention. You give it. A job needs to be completed. You do it.

One more act of kindness a week will add 52 moments of inspiration to your year. Push it to two a week and you add more than 100. Imagine the possibilities.

212° commitment

Indulge your good side once more each week. Start now.

The weather.

The traffic.

My boss.

My customer.

My mother.

My father.

Cease
to complain

My sister.

My brother.

I don't have enough ... But I really need ...

I can't ... If only [he, she, they] would ...

It's been a tough [day, week, month] ...

It's [Monday, Tuesday, Wednesday, Thursday, Friday] ...

212° approach

Be. Move forward. Cease to complain.

Your words move others. Your words move you.

Make yours send everyone in the right direction.

Complaining once less a day chokes off 365 seeds

of negativity a year.

212° commitment

Put a smile in the path of a complaint ... once daily.

Cease to complain.

Pause
and reflect

You skim the material.

"Great stuff."

"Really makes sense."

"I like that a lot."

You move on.

Quickly.

212° approach

You read the material. You pause. You reflect. You give it thought. Deeper thought. You embrace it or toss it aside but you do so after pausing — after reflecting on it for more than an inattentive moment.

Thought is important because it is thought that generally precedes action.

Pausing and reflecting — investing thought beyond an instant twice more each week on a particular topic creates more than 100 additional possibilities of action and/or improvement each year.

212° commitment

Pause and reflect — deeper — twice weekly.

Prune
the
diversions

When did you last evaluate the tasks you do every day

against what's most important to you?

When did you last evaluate them against who's

most important to you?

You have goals.

You have time.

You have energy.

Where should it be invested?

212° thought

Removing just two diversions from your life each week eliminates more than 100 distractions a year from what's most important to you.

212° commitment

Prune the diversions. Twice weekly.

Risk.
Attempt.

Comfort. Risk.

Both are enjoyable.

One we strive to create. One we try to minimize.

One can make us lazy. One can make us stronger.

When did you last risk failure?

When did you last leave your comfort zone?

212° challenge

Step out of your comfort zone at least once each week and create over 50 additional opportunities for excitement, challenge, and possibility each year. This is what life's about.

212° commitment

Risk. Attempt. Fail. Succeed. Once more each week. It's been said that youth is wasted on the young. By taking risks, we assure ourselves that life isn't wasted on the living.

Involvement and reminders drive continual awareness. And with awareness comes responsibility and action.

Let the number 212° serve as your constant reminder. It's your new way of thinking — your new way of acting. Write it down and leave it wherever it might serve you best — wherever you may need a prompt to extra action (or just action itself) ... your bathroom mirror ... the dashboard of your car ... in your "cube" at work ... on your refrigerator ... above the door of your workout room.

It's time
to turn up the
heat!

Go to work.

Mac Anderson

MAC ANDERSON is the founder of Successories, Inc., the leader in designing and marketing products for motivation and recognition. Successories, however, is not the first success story for Mac. He was also the founder and CEO of McCord Travel, the largest travel company in the Midwest, and part owner/VP of sales and marketing for Orval Kent Food Company, the country's largest manufacturer of prepared salads. Mac's accomplishments in these three unrelated industries provide some insight into his passion and leadership skills.

Mac brings the same passion to his speaking and writing. He speaks to many corporate audiences on a variety of topics, including leadership, motivation, and team building.

He has written three books: *The Nature of Success*, *The Power of Attitude*, and *The Essence of Leadership*, and has coauthored *To a Child, Love is Spelled T-I-M-E*, *The Dash*, and *The Race*. Mac also recently launched Simple Truths, a company publishing corporate gift books to reinforce core values.

For more information, please visit **www.simpletruths.com**

Sam Parker

Sam Parker is a cofounder of MaxPitch Media, Inc.
(www.maxpitch.com) — publisher of justsell.com,
the web's resource for sales leaders,™
and other content for business leaders.

A native of the Washington, D.C., area, he now lives
in Richmond, Virginia, with his wife Jennifer (an artist)
and their three children.

He can be reached with feedback or to discuss
speaking engagements at **sam@justparker.com**.
On the web, he continues to explore the details of life
and business at **www.justparker.com**

Great Gift Books...

...For Your Employees and Your Customers.

If you have enjoyed this book and wish to order
additional copies; or if you would like to learn more about
our full line of beautifully designed corporate gift books,
please visit us at www.simpletruths.com, or,
call us toll free at (800) 900-3427.

Please note that our books are **not sold in bookstores,
Amazon or other retail outlets.** They can only be
purchased direct from Simple Truths or a
Simple Truths distributor.

We look forward to serving you.

Call (800) 900-3427 or visit www.simpletruths.com

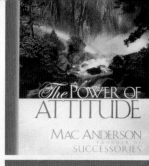

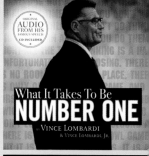

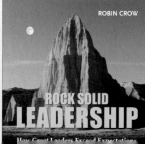